BLACK
RIBBON

A COLLECTION OF POEMS

JUSTIN GOODE

CONTENTS

A Mental Health Awareness Poem

Dear Bestfriend

Before I heard the term mental health
I fell in love with contradictions
Made love to split decisions
If the evens turned odd
I would split legs to new dvsn
All my standards came in doubles
Anxiety kept me rushing
My life was a puzzle
Of a hundred missing meanings
Incomplete and complete as I compete for some virtue
Kind hearted and hot tempered
Too cordial and too dismissive
Focused on everything
While
Trusting losing something
Is losing nothing
Even if something is some structure
You know
Fear none
Love less
It would be easier for me to function
Before I heard the term
It was you trippin
Ease your mind get some pussy
Ease your mind pour some henny
Ease your mind roll them woods up
Ease your mind nigga hold up

Before I heard the term it was
You think you trippin?
You ain't trippin like that nigga
You think you got it bad?
I got a cousin that can't walk with you
I got a sister that can't talk with you
Nigga even I got a condition and I can still kick it wit
you

Before I heard the term
I thought you stayed heathy by running
At least three times a day
Two steps towards conflict
One step towards peace then you walk away
Just like everybody else
I thought you stayed healthy
By running
Cause it helps you breathe
By thinking about something else
I thought you stayed healthy by takin your mind off
yourself
Not in
Just out
Cause what's out
Now
Belongs to somebody else
Before I heard the term mental health
I can't lie
I thought about it first
It was too easy to roll off the tongue
Like it seemed familiar like I seen it before

In driveways in uncles in siblings
Like I seen it before
In friends in family in commitment
Like I seen it before
In my own eyes
In my own pride
I can't lie
It's like
Like I had thought about it before
It was too easy like this definition crosses my mind in
real time
With real whys
A real guide
Not illness
Just the result when your existence starts to peak
Really it's the duality of niggas
Look inside
See the calm and the and the wildness in niggas
Look in time
You can see the conflict in niggas
Is it
Environment vs self
Ego vs self
Protection of oneself
Before I heard the term mental health
I knew I could change the world
After I heard it
I knew
What was healthy for me comes first
No matter what
You have to do what's best for you first

No matter what
Cause
It's your point of view on issues
No matter what
I can never look at you different
The same way you might see a man with principles in prison
The same way you may see idols mix wisdom with liquor
The same way you may see the brave take flight as a decision
The same way your ego might ask you to swap out money for morals
And my instincts never hesitate
Nigga really what's the issue
Cause lately my lady is my justice
And she
Talkin like she can't find peace
Like there's some kind of conflict going on
Like if it ain't then why I'm never coming home
Silence is golden
As my eyes drift to a gaze
And my hand finds a pencil
And the pencil finds it a page
And I realize
Maybe it's me
I'm tripping
Times like this
Remember
Don't forget to be your own best friend
So today

I give you my mantras and my positive affirmations
As I forget my past flaws and move forward in
progression
I see my life's passion has forced me to face a past
trauma that I two times neglected
So this is my word from saviors
That will help my people who suffer from depression

Remember
It's how you talk to yourself that defines you
Sometimes you have to
Be your own best friend
Best friend
Please tell the truth even when your voice shakes
Don't forget what a village looks like
Don't forget what your village looks like
Don't ever forget about your family
From blood to sand
From friends who memories date back farther than
calendars can
Learning to never put bad energy on bad energy
Learn
Before you mention hurt
Remember peace
Learn
That you have to take time for yourself
Learn
To keep everything in place
Earn
The truth in every statement that you make
Turn

To new leafs
And new pages
Never your back on your own patience
Burn
Bad ideas
Not bridges
Learn
To take Fake forgiveness
Fall
Into the pleasure of forgiveness
Vick's
For hard decisions
Psalms
For repentance
Gossip less
Enjoy your space
Talk to God
Walk with faith
Weigh your options
Not your problems
And as you travel from worry to work
Redefine it
See it as
Travel between your position and your title
Travel to new beaches
Remember there's time for solace
But
No man is an island
It's always time for confidence
But pride can be a problem
Wait

Best friend
Don't forget what you came for
What you woke up for
What you need more for
What you see when your eyes are closed
The spaces and places to unlock doors
To empty rooms
That look long left abandoned
And when the time comes don't forget to speak
When you speak
See whose surrounded
It's the brave faces that can bring you peace
The same peace that's inside you
It's always what's inside you
But wait
Listen
Best friend
Your voice didn't shake

CHAPTER 1

THE BOND

Bless youStranger

Sometimes I feel like we might need more love
Like it needs to stick in the air more
Like it needs to be in every moment
Every time
Like it needs repetition
Like it's a practice
Like we might need more practice
Cause in time it tells
It tells it's own truth
Cause in every dialogue that turns to food for thought
you should see
Just like before every meal you eat
You might need to pray first
It helps with your appetite that way
For some reason this food now feels safe
Cause for some reason love is on my plate
And in my face
Its apart of me
Wanting to be contagious

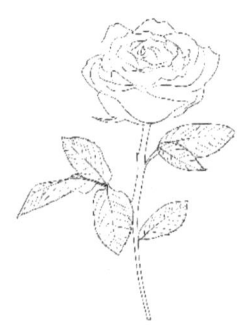

Heirloom

Too many times
I seen a woman be a stepping stool
How odd
God helping men get a rise
God sacrificing for man
Preparing for life and forsaking the one who gives it
Eating in Eden and hoping God is real
Like it must be something in the sky still
Like it's not right in front of you
Like what if God taught me and I taught her
What if
In all days and most days
In all nights and most evenings
What if
Everything you ever knew was all there was to believe
Like the way you believe in me
And she hold truths that I can't make on my own
That me you and peace is the holy trinity
Like sometimes I can't be sober to know the truth
Like sometimes I have to be drunk off you
Like praise
Is something you should know
The things I already have memorized
Like of all the moments
I fell in love with ours the most
Like just how woman made us human
She can make us holy again

And She Said

Be careful baby I need this trust to breathe
I know it's hard on the outside but inside its fragile
indeed
They say it's clinical
But it's not to me
It does more than pump blood
It gives life to me
That vital piece

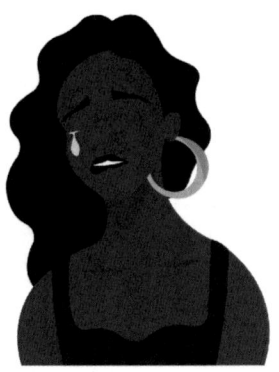

And He Said

These things don't come with directions
You don't assemble man or woman
No you don't build companions
You don't give a ring for good luck
You don't give a knee when guessing

You jus don't

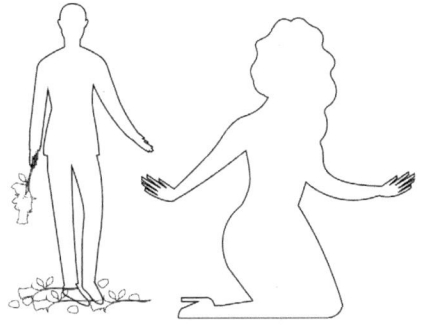

Before the Break-Up

Our voices echoing the same thing
Why'd you get so close just to hurt me
Why I got to hear hateful word from the person that
loves me
How can the same lips that kiss curse me
Giving you my worse
But when you walk away you take the best of me
All of me

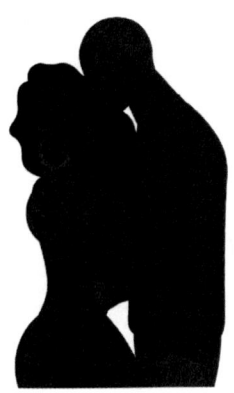

Comets

We deserve rain sometimes
Even the brightest stars see rain sometimes
See they never mention that
In science class
That comets break down
They lose acceleration
In the same speed of life that flashes before your eyes
They get dim
Everything loses its sparkle at some point
You see even comets have dreams when they're racing
It's hard to tell cause we only see them once maybe twice in
a lifetime
and each story told sounds the same
It came how it went
In a flash that absorbed your eyes
That stuck to your skin and shivered your souls
That flashes in the dark when you put on blind folds
It's different
When your spirit animal is actually a flying rock
That you only seen once
But you know because you shared the same dreams
That same dream that you can be a planet too
With culture and food and homes and views
You could be a planet too
With rivers and valleys and mountains and charm
You could be a planet too
With deserts and weeds and personality and trees
If you could ever stop racing after nothing
And
Just sit back and breathe

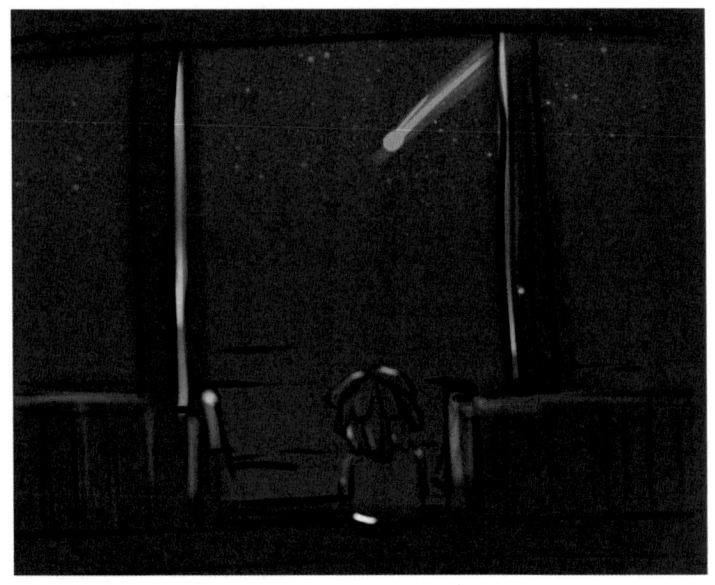

I only want you
And I can only get that from you
And I love that

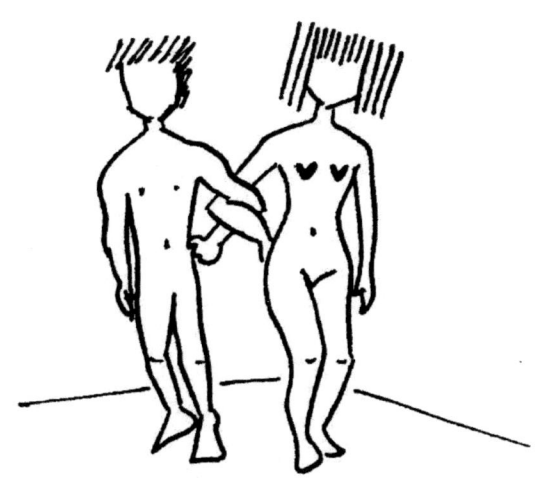

A Real Rose

Everyone has that one aunt
That has a smile like the rainbow
But eyes that look like its rained all night
And you can tell when it showered because
underneath
You can see the clouds stuck around
Or or or
That one aunt who had that memory
Randomly roll down her cheek
And land in her lap
And as soon as she wipes it away
You can tell she still wants it back
Or or or
That one aunt who uses blush for bruises
And concealer mixed with black and purple
And you beat her boyfriend
And you're still mad because it took for you to see it
for her to feel noticed
Her black is beautiful too you know
For that colored girl her black is beautiful too you
know
Not black and blue her black is beautiful too you
know
You got to fight for love but baby don't let it whoop
you; you know

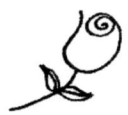

Facts

When are we going to realize that hearts are jus as
valuable as diamonds
And see that the world rotates enough to put two
souls in alignment
And when the wind blows in love
The melody is equivalent to wind chimes and sirens
Corset kissed hips
And rings that unify that balance
And the old scars from heart break
Are replaced by hickies from affection that never gets
tired
And insight that mature love is the only situation to
ever bring a child in
And endurance enough to know you can never grow
old together
If you never put the time in

1st

That's when she told me
I just want to lay with you
But baby I spent enough nights to know I can't spend
another day with you
I don't know about our future
But our past is a faded picture
Reminiscing on faded tears and smeared makeup
You catching the hiccups when your temper start to
pick up
And
Me feeding you lies til you screaming that you fed up
And
The taste of you on my lips every time that we met up
The fear in your eyes every time that we made up
Hard feelings and soft hearts
See
Making love is a lost art and
I use to find it in you at night
I think that's why I use to go raw in you at night
But
Don't worry about them other bitches
Baby you know I want you as my wife
She said that's the problem nigga
I can't see you as a great husband no matter how long
I keep you in my life
And that's why I cant lay with you
Cause I spent enough nights to know I can't spend
another day with you
Idk about our future but our past is a faded picture

I thought this is when people ran
To get back in shape
After they let themselves go
After they forgot too often
After they let things settle in
I thought this is when people ran

Behold a Lady

I never had a relationship last longer than a tattoo
Like
A woman made from ink
Like
A woman permanent like ink
Like
A woman stained to me
Pertinent
Determined
Compassionate
Like a woman
Like a woman made with a gun

Words From a Feminist

She said
These men they want to police my body
After I was false idled
After they worshipped my body
She said
These men want to censor my body
After they undressed my body
After they professed custody of my clit
And limped back and said tell me baby that pussy is
mine
And begged for nudes
And after we broke up threatened to leak as if taking a
picture was a crime
And then I said tell me more
And she professed it with time
She said these men they won't police my heart
They won't protect and serve my heart
They won't acknowledge wrong doings when they're
shooting
And when their actions are the reason it's falling apart
And the pieces…they just lay there
She paused
And said
Do you know why he's my ex-boyfriend
If you look at his hands
There are no cuts on them
Because he never took the time to pick up the parts
And told me he heard I fucked ten men
So go tell them

Let them be the ones to keep digging your parts
She said
That's the problem with men
There's no science in the things that they do
I let too many see my clitoris now you avoid my
uterus
I didn't know being casual could make you abandon
my womb

Dallas Buyers Club

Her life is like the sequel to the Dallas buyers club
Fuck love
After telling the truth she can barely get a hug
Medicine is life saving
Dabbing between pills of biotin and Dr Sebe
Alkaline fruits and kindred spirits
She got to admit everything she been through every
time a man get her pussy pulsating
Yea you the shit
I don't know if I want to risk my life on this
Reminisce of jokes from Eddie Murphy
Putting your dick on the crap table
Don't know if I'm gone roll the dice like this
She humbled
Back to patience
Another free spirit in the party
At home there's no man waiting
You know her pussy dirty but her soul clean
And enough heart to battle anything

Cold Blue

This is for the souls made of diamonds cause pressure
wasn't enough
For those who surround loyalty with kindness
And fatally attracted to distrust
Those who Confuse Black love
With oil love
That pipe line love
That destroys culture
Homes
Sanity
That build monuments of ego
Pain
And tragedy
That love that feels rich
But it stains you
It pays you
The same way that it plagues you
As the world screams we need an alternate source
We need a light love
That's not gone with the wind
That solid love
That doesn't change for a friend
It builds
Patios not walls
It feels secure
But open is the door of the vault
It's the the cure for paranoia
Of where have you been
It fills voids
Of the please don't ever text me agains
It holds hands

Into the sunset
That your eyes drift to
It is both naked and clothed
Only the lover can tell you which is true
It's the mustard seed that sits next to the mountain
That you had to push through
It's so eager to please
That's why we say I do
It's so eager to knees
For situations we pray through
We love love
We hold love
We want love
The only question is who are you making it to

Priceless

This goes past the definition of distance
Filled this void so long
I didn't realize you was missing
Reality hits
My world crashes down
Just to see bridges's built with love
Engulfed in flames
Reiterations of words filled with curse
Humming
If you loved me
You would pay attention
If you paid attention
You would know my worth
Now I got regret as some wood
I got
Pain as a ladder
As I build monuments of forgiveness
While I convince you that that bridges never mattered
Jesus was a carpenter
Maybe he could build a pedestal
I got to take a look in the mirror
It's something different going on
I got pussy on my phone
While I tell you to hold on
I tell you to be strong
But why I got to be so fuckin stubborn
Why I got to mix cheating with my loving
Why I got to destroy while I build
Why can't I learn to forgive

Why can't I be honest about this still
Why I got to convince you to love me
When I showed you
I didn't love you first
Why I feel sympathy for the people that I hurt
Why your truth sound like a curse
Maybe you're right
If I love you
I'd pay attention
If I paid attention
You wouldn't have to convince me of your worth

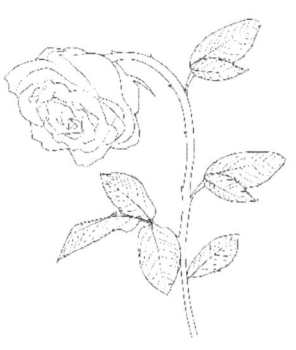

Still Cheering

Did you know I was still cheering
Even while you were still healing
Going back and forth
With yourself
And I'd still listen
Still gripping
On
To our past and future
Like a vibe to still music
Did you know I was still cheering
Like go a little longer
Go a little stronger
Let's celebrate then keep going
I was still cheering
Even if it was from the crowd
Even if I knew we would never last
Even if you never forgive me
Did you know I was still
Calling your name
after I ignored your calls
After I
Wouldn't take the blame
Was asking for a draw
Instead of a second chance
Even when we didn't stand a chance
I was still cheering
Even while you were still healing
Going back and forth
With yourself

And I'd still listen
Still holding
To what truly matters
And that's you and your dreams
For the things that really matter
Even if I'm not on the other end of the smile
Even if
My voice goes hoarse
God gave me a choice
And the decision is human
To not give in or give up
Jus to keep my voice up
I was still cheering
With frogs in my throat
My butterflies started to joke
I never stopped cheering

In everything that I do
In everything that I am
It's me at all times
And that's what I have to offer you
In full
And it only comes in halves when it's emptied
And you
You tell me I'm empty
Like I can't pour any more
Like you checked first
Like you made sure before you told me
I remember
From a young man
And from souls before me
And bestowed upon me
Tyranny of women
The weariness of women
The mystery of women
That was solved by few
And spoken by many
And I knew
It was the eyes you have
That see what they wish
That move how they wish
That make judgements for you
Cause all that is seen by the eye
Is never true of the spirit

What if you fell in love with diving
Into the selves of you
And repeated you
Til you seen the depths
Of An ocean or a well
Or does it have a city inside
An Atlantis of men and women
Stumbling across cobblestone

Abstract affection

I love the plainness in you
Dress you down to nothing
And plan this with you
No need to search the whole planet it's you
My ego convinced me to tell you the truth
Your love gets me light headed
And
As the tree in my life grows
I know
You planted my roots

It's the same way
All over again
Make you fall in love all over again
Make you hold your breathe all over again
Make me want to hold you all over again
And again
Like loving repetition is loving you
It went so well the first time I don't mind doing it
again

In the day that you met love
And the day you learned how to speak it
That time in between
Helps build definition

Love Was A Sin

If love was a sin then I'd burn in hell like it was
heaven sent
And thank God for the blessing that he cursed me
with
See if love was a sin then I'd burn in hell like it was
heaven sent
Jus let me keep the ring so I'll forever know what
commitment meant
If love was a sin

Those legs that once belonged to a brothel I'll commit
to the pair
Look in the mirror the reflection is of one dangerous
man
Know that it's salvation if I indulge once
It's damnation if I care
She's five foot you choose she's standing astute
Those eyes fixated on temporary lust
I'm enchanted by you
Her curves carved in arches
Her skin stained in the most beautiful hue
God's design mixed with the Devils work of art
Provoking the flesh of being confused
You see
To me to only touch once would be a crime in itself
I'm willingly accused
I can see my heart in her self
Intuition speaks she's feeling it to
From fucking to love making to saying I do

When hearts merge they catch fire the saying is true
You see
In this case we're hexed trading salvation for love
But long as I'm burning in hell I'm grateful that I'm
burning for us
You see

Cause if love was a sin then I'd burn in hell like I was
heaven sent
And thank God for the blessing that he cursed me
with
See if love was a sin then I'd burn in hell like it was
heaven sent
Just let me keep the ring so I'll forever know what
commitment meant
If love was a sin

We are all trying to fight the physical
The same way that we fight age
Defy it
The same we would do to gravity
To float to new plateaus
To measure ourselves in different accords
To find new mediums in the art of our lives
To gather and breathe
We find solace in who we are
And time does that
Luckily we are met with people
And these people
With different shapes and sizes and intentions
They have found a way to define us
To the perspective of actions
And I'm not your father
But your lover
So I'm only going to tell you this once
I love you
And that's why I want the best for you
Cause great things happen daily
I want you to tell you that you are beautiful
And I love you
I want to tell you that you are worthy
And I love you
And know when all women of earth finally met
Many moons ago
In circumstances undefined
It was the black woman
In all shapes and sizes and shades
That in unison we all proclaimed

That if we came from earth
Then we came from her
And for that we gave the power to men
So I came to tell you the truth again

Silence breaks stares
As the time to speak has yet to come
I miss you
And I miss you
Sure enough
Laying down is the best way to keep in touch
It's a must
Our greetings seem different
Holding hands
Kiss and touch
Our mornings are themed different
At your best
You are love
Her
Body language speaking in peace
So she
Likes me
Coffee
And Miguel in the morning
While time stands still
But for some reason hands are still roaming
Now look at this
Tu es ma paix
Her body language speaking in French
Corset dipped hips
And ripped la Perla
As a ocean runs from your river to the sofa
Baby
Don't mind me in the water
It's already tremors in the living room
Baby

I cant be mad about some water

If you
Raise your voice
Falsettos would be in order
While you still claim that we don't speak enough
But
Sure enough
Laying down
Is the best way to keep in touch
Let's just
Keep our breathing in sync
For the next hour
Bring to reality
Everything that you think
And swear
And curse
And eyes rolling back
Baby

It's always worth
It's always worth
The attitude

CHAPTER 2

THE CHAOS

Free the Slaves

The pride in me desegregated
In front of my eyes I see
My liberty as a free man
I still never helped free a man
They got niggas in my back yard turning into stock I
see
I got to help you beat the odds I see
The God in me
Turned its back
Gave a side eye to me
You unlearned all that bullshit
Jus to see the next man take the same route
I see
Can't interject
Can't break the cycle I see

New Cinema

Don't you love your slasher movies
When the villain has a machete
And the machete takes what it wants
And all knives and villains get away
And the police heard of him
Maybe seen him
But they can't catch him
It might have been self defense
Who doesn't have a mask
Who doesn't have a knife
Who hasn't been afraid
Who hasn't got away
Don't you just love your slasher movies
Where people jus die at random
Where every time you see the body
Nobody can call the cops
Where every time they are screaming louder
And nobody can ever tell what's wrong
Where every time feet keep moving faster
But nobody's really getting far
Don't you love your slasher movies
Where the killers name is hidden but right in front of
you
Where they never say the name of the person they are
killing
Where's there's no traffic and time stands still
The scenario is so easy for your life to slip away
It's the perfect time
In the perfect place

For men with hate
And drive
And a plan
And a reason
And a decision
That we've all seen
The logic that comes from murder
Flash across our screen again

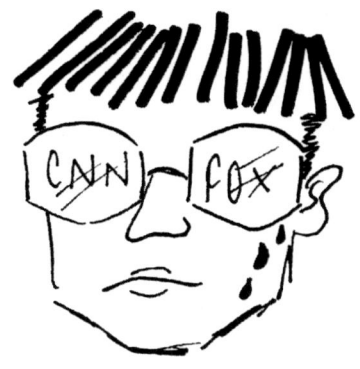

The black man must be god
How else
Would he never treat others how you treat him
How else
would he forgive and not forget

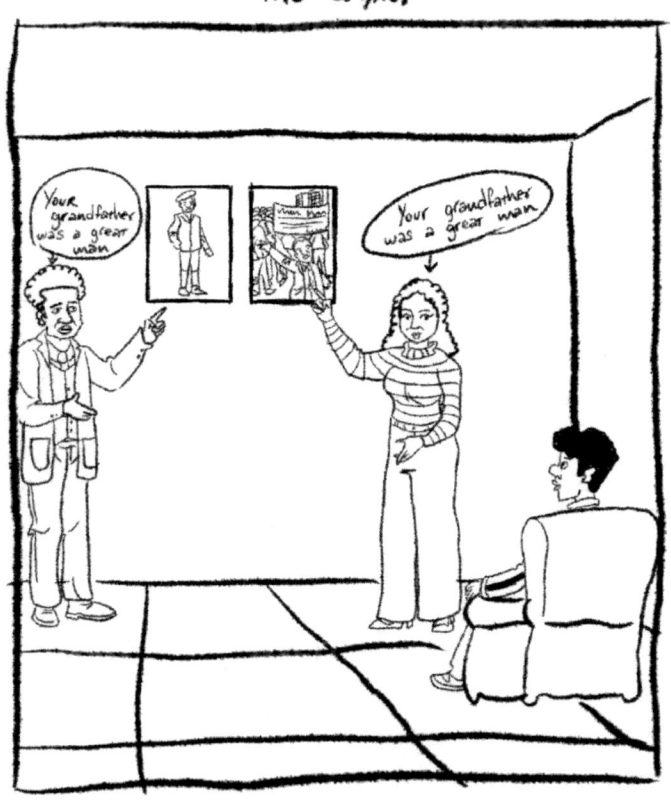

My spirit believes in God
But my flesh
But it's like my flesh
Believes in time travel
Like if I could find the right pieces
Like technology has come so far
Like I seen it in movies
Like it's so much easier to go back than it is to move
forward
Like this can be awkward
To see the past in 20/20
To see the misguided make decisions
To see procrastination from a window
To see your own body refuse to grow old
And still the trouble in its wishes
But still it's like
My spirit believes in God
But my flesh believes in time travel
Like it likes to record
So it would be so much better to go back and look at
the live tapes
Like it would be so much better to do it all over again
In person
The same person
With new answers
Like this is how you make things different
This is how you make a difference
Like this is the only right decision
Like my flesh can see what legacies do
Like it knows
Before I shed more dead weight
Look back

Still seeing black clouds
Still seeing disbelief in a black child
Still see opinions run wild
Still seeing you
While they mimic you
And say you never made it
Claiming they are God's favorite
While they sway in God's favor
Maybe you're unearthly
Sent from the moon and the stars
Skin stained with the suns lovingly scars
Maybe it's cause
And effect
Or maybe we don't live the same
Maybe our closets are different
Ours has bones while there's has monsters in it
The force that moves
Until they feet push them to prejudice
Until they are seeing you
While everyone they love
They mimic you
And they say you never made it
They say your body is vacant
And that your soul is no longer earthly
That it sways in God's favor
I know you are God's favorite
Sent from the moon and the stars
And your
Skin was stained with the suns lovingly scars
Every time we tell the story
Jus know

The truth is involved
The real question is
Where do we go from here
Was justice jus a trend
Where do we go with fear
Why are we pointing fingers
While they are pointing pistols
Why are you afraid
And not ashamed

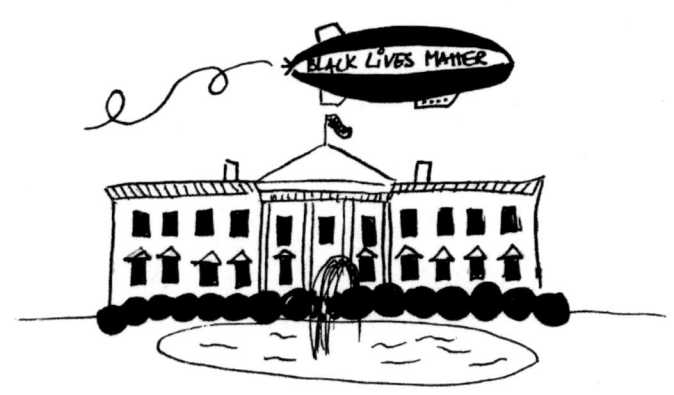

The 5th amendment
The Rights of Persons

That's why I give my heart and soul to those who
protesting for a lost life now
That inspiration bringing life round
I see it now
Long live the soul of James Brown
You got to walk around this bitch like I'm black and
I'm proud
Long live the soul of Georg Floyd
I know I'm raising 100k dollars worth of hell
But fuck it
They burned more
Long live the soul of Breana Taylor
I'm marching for you you better know
My heart and soul still goes to every black woman
across the globe
God give power to the land now
For every one who submitted
When they said black boy lay down
So many people got killed
In every county yea it's real
Now can we give living a chance now
Got to make it apart of your plans now
If the cops kill a man with his hands down
Now we got to get the FBI to come in
To help get they hands down?
Then fuck it
Add it to the list of my demands now
And if you want to speak to me about being equal

Come to me with your hands down
With some manners in your presence
With some respect in your voice
Like your talking to a man
Like your talking to a woman
Like your talking to a boy
Like your talking to a girl
Like your talking to me
On this land
That is birthed from my turmoil
That grows trees from my blood
Whose leaves use to call our names
Those of us who have seen a lynching before
And can make sure there will be no more

It was the misdirection that made me write
That push and pull of what my spirit wanted and
what the world offered
The world was so black and white once my
imagination died
That I had to bring color to the dying pictures around
me
The faces mauled with poverty
The seemingly endless cycle of Darwinism
The clinging to hope that all humans faced
And the catastrophe that is the truth
They all came in the form of a ribbon
And I wore that ribbon
For God heard me call for a cause
And gave me you

THE ADVENTURE OF COOTIE BROWN
The BarberShop

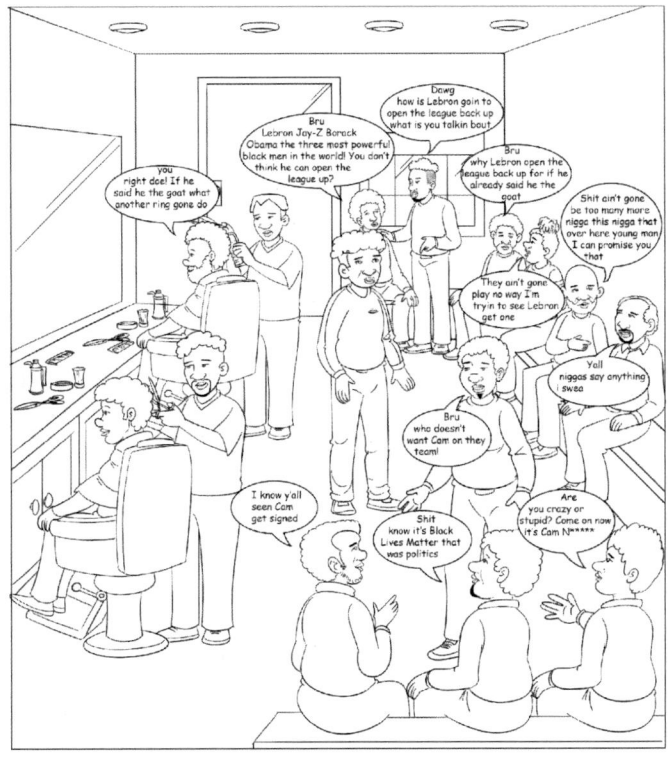

True trauma
Is self inflicted
the chaos you put on yourself
The victim and the culprit
Wondering on when your soul split
Daydreaming on time spent
Day to night
Nights to years
Years to tears
Eyes still windows to the soul
In every stare there's a code
In the mirror I can't hold
I jus
I jus can't trust me

The County

~~Juggs~~ still tempting
Even for a second
Pretending
As my niggas play rich in pictures
Watch as
Portrait mode makes 5k look like 50
And the question still is
Really whose workin
This year the comments might be more important than
the person
So
If you knew better you'd do better
As habits weigh more than purpose
But still
Man to man
Black to black
There's some shit I don't want to hear
About boys who turned animal cause stripes have
appeared
But still
Man to man
Black to black
There's some shit
That I don't want to hear
About
How you killed a black man and gave these crackas
twenty years
Like life is a priority
I know everything sits on a tier

As I'm
Watching women fight for abortion and fighting back
tears
But still
Theres some shit
I'm always gone hear
The stories of envy
How
Respect disappeared
How doggy's ears pop up when pussy is near
Ain't no bullets and ballets no more
It's either the bark or the bite
Ain't no loyalty no more
It's who with it tonite
Ain't no
Reason
To tell me that shit I can already hear
It echoes
From Fairhaven to
Thomas Road
It echoed
So
Everybody from Garden Walk to Tara knows
Victor Hill will
Give you weekend jail
Before he would ever let you go
And
If his girl is trippin
He'll catch a body and they'll
Still let him go
With that alone

How can we grow
All the soil been replaced with red clay
Where do we go
Play scared or play safe
Never played much
But I just keep hearing
Wise words from
Old
Women
A man should
Stay in a mans place
Words are power
You
Should never say much
Beware of cowards
And you must be a fool
To think if they don't have a lot
Then they don't want much
Demand your power
Remember
A man should stay in a mans place
So
Peace be peace nigga
And watch as strength mimics me
As my city is known if you come on vacation
You gone leave on probation or in the bing
Peace be peace
My nigga
What happened to serenity
Why we never seen it
Like my eyes can't see that

Like we can't lay there
We can't sleep in it
We can't be with it
Like our partners don't have it
It's not in our jobs
It's not in our life
It's not in our walk
It's not in our conversation
What happened to serenity
Was it made for me
Like is our skin is addicted to turmoil
My nigga
Peace be peace
As I go to war with everybody
Even the ones who look jus like me
What happened to us
Why does everybody feel like we not here
Like we can't be seen but only in one light
Nigga
Is this why we all want to be real
Instead of being real men
Or a real brother
Or a real friend
You stressing over Gucci
Nigga poverty is real
It last longer than 3 months
Detached?
Nigga why would I feel
If you touch me you might see I'm actually real
If you speak to me

You could see that you don't got to spend money to
get a point across
The good news is
Niggas stopped fronting they won't even wear a cross
But if they lying
They lying
Watch what they say
But I know
A boys words
Will walk a man to his grave
And I know
Your parents voice in your head
Has to be replaced
With your own
It has to happen on your own
So we can see who is really the enemy
Half the time
They look like we
In our circle
Shook they own hands
Gave respect to envy
And took another glance
And when they speak it sounds different
That's how I know
A boys words
Will walk a man to his grave
You got to replace that voice
Put a little bass in it
Give it some maturity
Give it some insight
It can no longer be innocent

But give it a little purity
Let it have a conscious
Love is heavy
Let it weigh in
Let's use different scales now
Be confused and find a way now

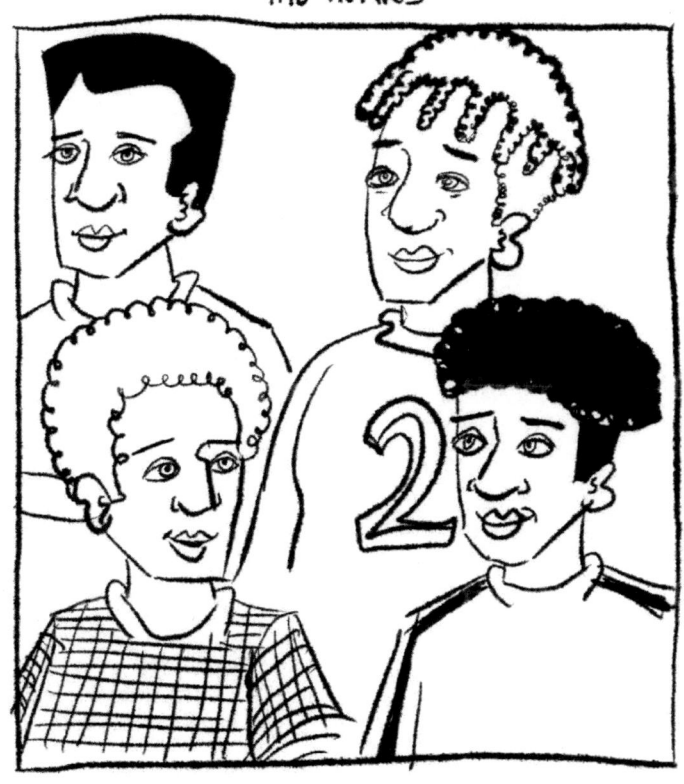

So humane that they thought you was docile
Black boy you're in public
Fight through pain and the willingness to act wild

Doggs & Birdds

Deep brushes caresses her curves
Star sprinkle the night sky where the moon is
observed
No introduction is needed
All that shit is absurd
Cause even God knows it's kind of hard to match a
dog and a bird
They say pity the fool
No I say pity be hers
She thinks cause I give her sex
That it's my affection that she truly deserves
But I'm roaming
And honestly that commitment shit be irking my
nerves
She says she love me
I swear that hurt me more than any four letter word
She says she need me
I swear that hurt me more than any four letter word
She says she trust me
And felt she was living when our hearts started to
merge
I told her I'm claustrophobic
In fear of close objects
And when you enter my world
See my walls stop to topple
And when you get on top
See my world feels honest
Now you're pouring out your feelings
Got dam just stop it

Live in the moment
Die in the past
Yes those memories hold true
But that flame never last
See this world here is mine
On that island you remain stranded
Then she replied back
Like Juice
How the fuck you break my heart single handed
I'm your wifey with no husband what kind of family
would you abandon
Your a King with no Queen what kind of caste can you
manage
 Why every time I get close that shit put you in a panic
You cut my heart deep is verbal abuse suppose to be
the bandage?
Words full of pain
Eyes full of sorry
Hands full of rage and she beat my chest hollow
I know I was coming at her sideways
But I want her by my side
I was acting like I liked her
So love was my facade
I was thinking with my dick
But in my heart the truth lies
It's hard to keep a woman in your bed
When your sheets are full of lies

After the world turned her back on her
How did she remain woman
How did her bones still move like woman
Her mouth still spoke like woman
Her whims jus as strong
Her heart jus as wide
Her life still left to be discarded
As easily as the breeze do
How did she still remain woman
If we think she can come
And go like that

THE ADVENTURES OF COOTIE BROWN

PART IV

THE WOMAN

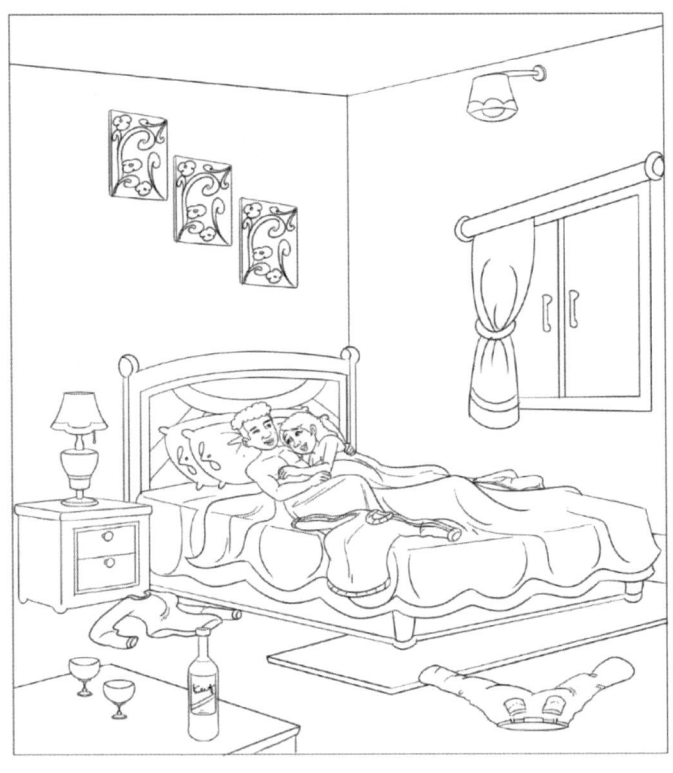

Love is too tricky
Cause it makes it too easy
To make you feel powerless with my decisions
It makes it too easy
To pick a side with best interest
These roles make it too easy
To decide I was finished
Cause if the tables were turned
And you could pay me back
With the loyalty that I've earned
You would rather turn your back and decide we was
finished

More Angels

That awkward moment when you soul searching and
you stumble across some demons
The coincidence when God gives you a mirror when
you're searching for someone to believe in
Blessed with enough imagination to reach for the stars
Still
Creative enough to make your own hell for no
apparent reason
Jus know It's taboo to have horns piercing from your
flesh still
Jeopardizing hurricanes for tornadoes
Mood swings when the wind blows
Trading a notebook for a halo
Salvation for a tempo
Bruised and battered morals running after a fragile
ego
That race never ends
Across the finish line it's dismantled situationships
and unbalanced friends
The root of all evil is equivalent to a means to an end
Dear Lord
If there's ever a moment when man starts to question
his worth
Bury his knees to the ground until he inherits the earth
Replace his wants with purpose
And his needs with whatever it's worth
And don't let him start living until he realizes it was a
blessing from birth

Peace God

God why you give me innocence
I can't leave this earth with it
Can't leave the church with it
Can't take it serious
Can't find no worth in it
Every time I show it
Somebody laughs and give it back to a nigga
It wasn't yours to keep
There's so much shame in Indian giving
God why did you give me innocence
I just use it when I'm being naive
Childish
Too secure with my trusting
When I throw away my instincts
Idk why but I do that shit on purpose
It helps burns the bridge I never built
It helps put a whole in the fence
It helps me feel the blows I was suppose to miss
I can admit it it helps me feel human again
God why
You did this on purpose
You did this with purpose
Make me feel full so I can pour into the empty
Make me seem like a fool so I can give them someone
to envy
Make me feel pulled so I can stretch out a century
Dear god make me giving again

Freed Slaves

Ask your forefathers how those shackles feel
3/5th of a man with a whole heart
Speaking a language he was forbidden to learn
Torn from a family he was built to destroy
And grew old and died
With a life he would never earn
Ask your forefathers how those shackles feel
Mother Africa; America has forged your bastard
In a trade where the boats don't turn backwards
Jump overboard with chants of hope to see the sharks
turn the ocean a reddish coat
For once you are bought your body has to pay its tole
And it's a lifetime of servitude for those you birth
To see the area of gray for the black life still tilts
between value and worth
Where there's a thin line between freedom and purge
Every time you say amen the pastor told you slavery
was heaven on earth
A field where a 100 year old man was still called a boy
And if that niggas fingers start to bleed then he's lazy
and we'll beat em til he's numb
And I wish a nigga would run cause yesterday we
hung one for fun
And when the shackles came off there were no boats
no maps and an ultimate fear not to swim
No tribes no solace
Just a new man with a new tongue

The Voyage

For those who didn't make it across the ocean
Bones never resting
Nestled in the gallows of the ocean
Stripped piece by piece
But property jumping overboard
It just looks unfortunate
It looks as if they didn't want their life
After a white man bought it for a small portion
It looks as if they were depressed
As if they were tormented from the trip
As if
They could swim back miles and miles from wince
they came
As if they woke to find themselves on a boat
As if they were never sold at all
But rather stolen

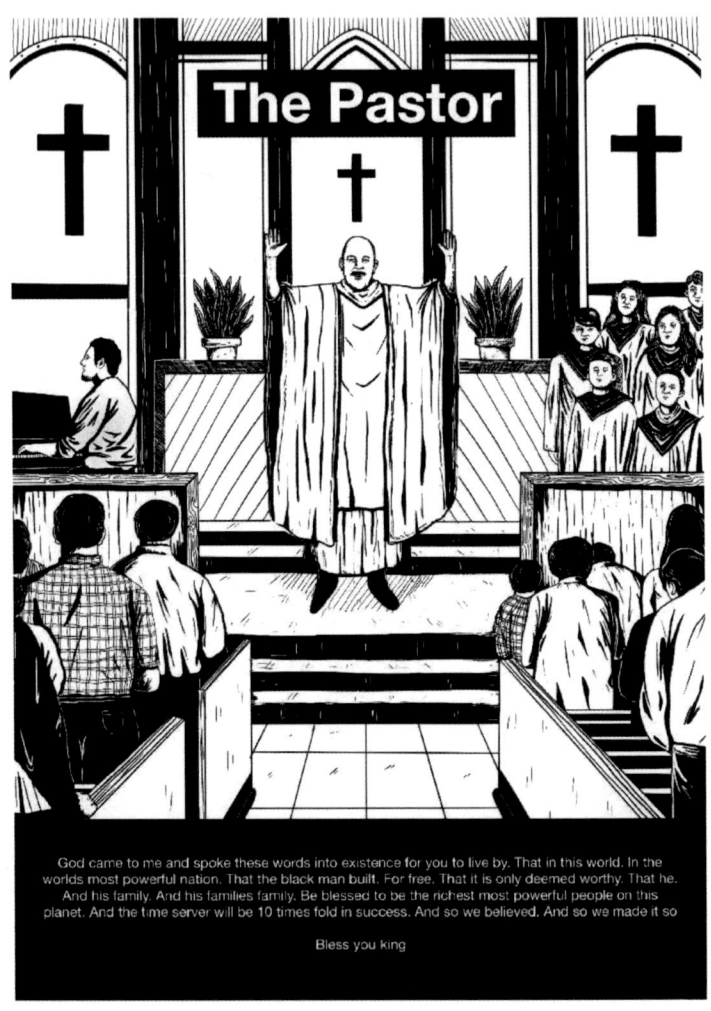

God came to me and spoke these words into existence for you to live by. That in this world. In the worlds most powerful nation. That the black man built. For free. That it is only deemed worthy. That he. And his family. And his families family. Be blessed to be the richest most powerful people on this planet. And the time server will be 10 times fold in success. And so we believed. And so we made it so

Bless you king

YOU MUST BE A FOOL TO THINK SLAVERY WAS THE START OF THINGS
BLACK MAN ORIGINALLY WERE KINGS

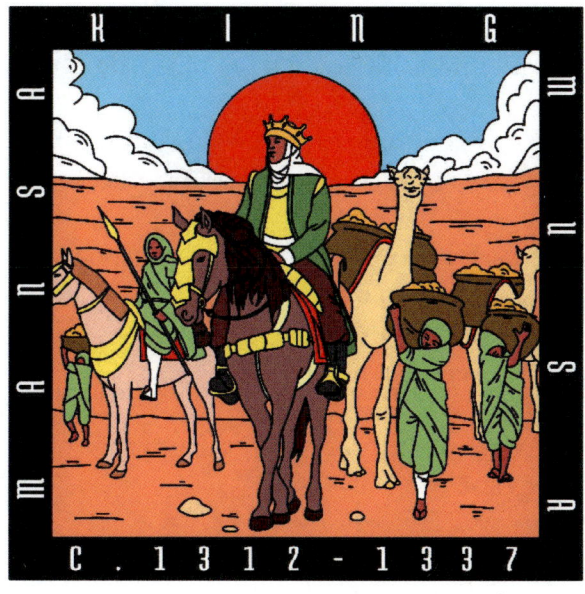

Modern Day Runaway

But don't cry when they lynch me
Hold to those memories on how all lives matter
And persuade black people how they should forgive
the man that erased our history
Borrowed cultures from present slaves
Racism is living proof that if hell was on earth
Black and White would be engulfed in different flames
Burn to different ashes even if we rose from the same
clay
Africa; a continent now synonymous with a state
Of the art way of diluted black bloods with certain
aid(s)
Welcome back to America where if you speak peace
they put a black man on a balcony
Cause a pedestal is no platform for a slave
Once he lies dead we'll pass a law
Give a day
And name a million streets in remembrance of his pain
That's the past
What have you done for me lately?
Police is back to their original agenda
Turning souls to trending topics
And court systems ensure that they'll always get away
But don't cry
Don't you cry
when they lynch me

Blessings

Psalms is poetry
And I formed it with my palms
As I put it on my arms
The beginning of it all
Like It's an experience for us all
Like at times my life seems biblical
Like today I seen Judas amongst my students
A fair fade but Jesus is my pupil
I gave him my heartache through fist and cuffs
I told him I was disappointed in him and didn't lift
him up
Reconciled with repentance
Then blessings became things
And I gave him 12 friends
And told him they will lift you up
But today
I seen Judas amongst my students
And my heart dropped
A snake a boy with no plans that shit never hit a soft
spot
But I taught him well let's see my sons thoughts
But he didn't speak
He showed you how to be weak
To keep a coward in your company to the point that
you sink
But it's all forgiven
I love all my little children
And as you know
No matter how many ass whooping's that I give them

They all don't listen
But they all my children
And I seen Judas this morning
Mourning
Lying about the fact that he didn't mean to disappoint
me
Saying he got us back
And that he was going to be anointed
And I sat there and grinned
Cause on top of the last you
You placed another sin
You see this
I can forgive cause I'm God
I should've seen less than you
Cause your skin paler than my sons
And that's odd
I taught him everything he know
He put his faith in you all
And I see you got some good in you
With a whole bunch of flaws
But you a got dam fool if you think I'm gone put a
snake in my yard

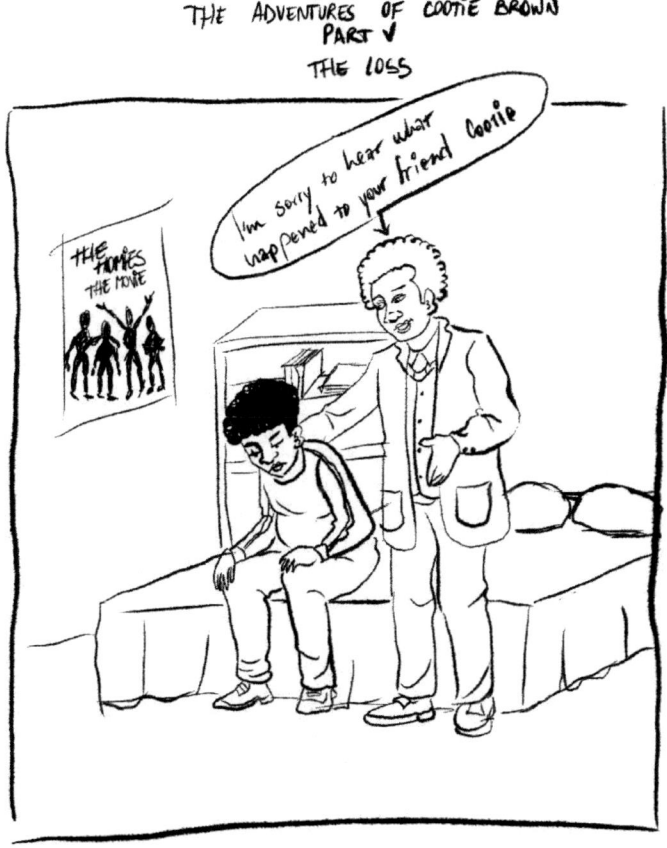

The Talented Mr. Ripley

I have an infinity for dying things
I love buying things that don't last forever
I can't put my finger on it
I can't put my lips on it
It's jus the continuum to me
How many times do you throw roses away til you see
the shit is boring
Til you realize the money doesn't cost too much
The time doesn't take too much
That the repetition in gifts can me limited
To the time you have
That memories fade with familiar faces
That the past is dementia

Black Man
They say it's nothing to you
But money and violence
Maybe a house
And that car that you like
And the clothes that you love
And the things you adore
And the things you ignore
And the things that you hide
But fuck it I got scars on my back too
They say us black men
There's nothing about us
But money and violence
With maybe a house
And that car that we like
And the clothes that we love
And the things we adore
And the things we ignore
And things that we hide
Like we were the first
To find meaning in our life
Just to find the world sees our life has no meaning
Like we can't have conversation
Like he wants peace
Give him stress
Get him vexed
Give him
Death
As they ignore the things they seen
In Kings
In the foot steps of slaves who opened doors

Those who left cages to open more
I never learned to judge you niggas
How can I
After I lost everything to niggas
Lost it all trusting niggas
Lost it all overlooking niggas
How can I
When I spent my whole life looking not to be afraid
To avoid self hate
Where today
Everything that a black man thinks is strong
Comes off as weak
Cause it's how we do it
Or what we do
Even if it's second
Especially if we are first
Especially if we are the only ones
Especially if we don't have money
Then we are a desolate gold mine
Meant to be pimped for less
The worlds only niggers
Now the world sees themselves as such
When did nigga become synonymous with underdog
Instead of free labor
When the us thing isn't a us thing
When it's an ally but not a us thing
It's jus

Third World Countries

What about the third world countries in North
Carolina
That through is his lack of acknowledgement that Pat
McCrory keeps jeopardizing
Everyday it's fuck Isis or Al Queda
Cause it's bloods and crips whose shooting niggas
before they could ever get a license
You know
That heartache you feel
Knowing black lives matter will never stop black
violence
From both sides
Cause some niggas are so numb from the world that
they won't hear it til that quote subsides
And these crackers
Don't give a fuck
They want to play both sides
What it do
Votes or revenue
Sometimes you can't even read in between the lines
To see this hidden truths
Some mu fuckas don't have a clue
What about the black youth?
Whether it be basketball or gangsta movies our first
ambition is to shoot
Sometimes I want to ask my future seed is it better to
be hard headed or naive

Or would you believe
If I told you the world take advantage of you cause
your innocent or your sweet
Or
If I told you there's no areas of gray
Either you're strong or your weak
Sometimes I want to ask
How do you break down things that you never seen
Like how do you label a girl as a whore
Just cause of where she sleeps
You see
She's been touched
So making love doesn't really mean the same thing
That's why she cringes every time you tell her to roll
over and take this D
Or
Label a man a criminal
Even though there's no
Food for thought
Or bread and water where he sleeps
What are you
A Street nigga
A Thug nigga
Abandoned through dope
Or orphaned off child support
It's no child left behind
Unless it's
A dope dealer slash hustler
Or black of course

It's synonymous
No time to see a psychiatrist
Just throw them in a cell and give them time to think
Really
What does poverty really mean
Low income
No love for a fatherless seed
No insight on what it means to live the American
Dream
No rent money
So the government gives you section 8
And republicans say you owe them one
So cliche
With your silver spoons
And your pots to piss in
With your twenty windows to choose a vision
And your millions of minorities to choose your victim
And the ambiguity that surrounds white privilege
And you're ignoring that people do more than
struggle
Ignoring that people are more prone to violence
When they are in the position to fight to live
And your mind state won't capture that thin line
between bars and freedom
And your mind won't capture that thin line between
pride and ignorance
And your mind won't capture that line between hope
and wishing

And your mind won't capture that thin line between
poetry and wisdom
But fuck that
This is for those righteous brothers who have a
likeness for sinning
Who know what a black man is but still won't despise
a nigga
For those who know what a queen but scream to the
world bitch why don't you forgive us
You see
Thats why
I have no times for them frauds who tell lies on wax
Get on stage and tell the truth
Let the people feel that
Put your demons in a notepad
Then let God touch that
And if that feeling is here
Then you know poetry is back

THE ADVENTURES OF COOTIE BROWN

THE FINALE

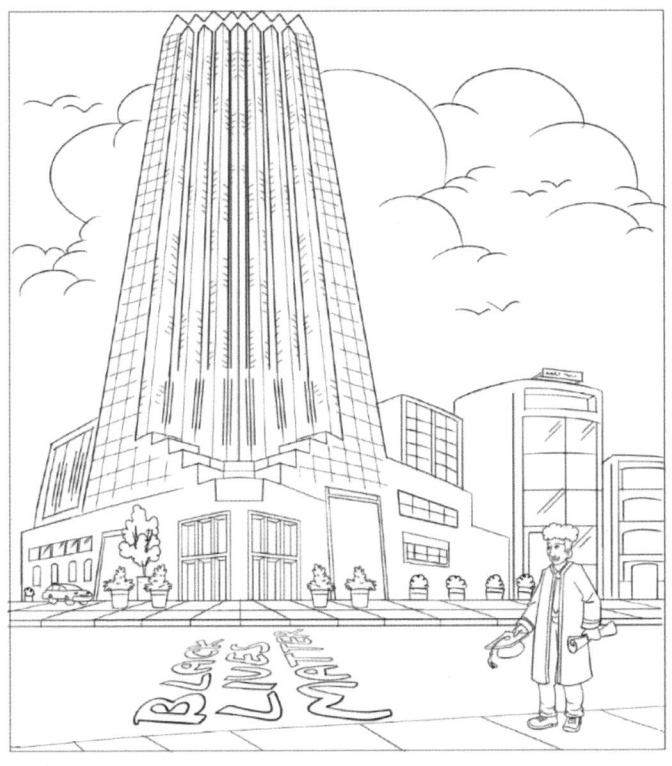

Chapter 3

The Still

Dear Ome
Breast Cancer Awareness Poem

It wasn't premonition when my skin started itching
I wanted it to stop
But really it was the beginning
Of days to come
And nights even worse
Where I'm praying for a cure
And scientist keep coming up short
I must be miracle in the making
Too much doubt keeps me vacant
Too much doubt when I'm naked
I know the devil made it but Jesus can you take it
Godly
Is how I'm seen in my mans eyes
He winks with his left
While a river rolls down his right eye
I know it takes a tribe to raise a child
But what scripture says
It takes a man praying on both knees to bring a
blessing to my life
He keeps saying it but I take it as a joke
But I love him for his hope
And he's patient with my health
It helps me be patient with myself
I don't feel so weak when I don't have to be strong by
myself
I know
It's the game of life
But it's too early to be cutting with them spades

And I got this theory
That my body is killing itself
Words are reality

I don't want to be a martyr to what I say
But I got this theory
That my body is killing itself
When I tell him he pulls me closer
But I just want to push away
Cause I got this theory
That my body is killing itself
See when my body breaks down my thoughts slip
away
I got this theory
When I say it out loud I really can't breathe right
I look at my wrist
Is this it's purpose?
I really can't see right
My mind playing tricks on me
I really can't think right?
I look at the hands in the clock
It's too late for the what if
So I put my theory to rest
And put my stress to the side
Give the glory to God
And promise to give it my best

Part 2

I prayed so long that the bruises on my knees keep
asking me
Please please please
You can't ask for forgiveness when you didn't do
anything
Whatever you do
Stop googling the difference between cancer and
disease
And see
That a busy mind can't keep track of what you love
and what you fear to believe
Besides
Did you try to a new joke
Like
This reminds me of the time that Nefertiti caught a
cold
Or
Did you try to telling the truth
Like
If it gets bad or gets worse I'm never letting go
Or
No
Did you try being positive
Like that gown looks good on you
Or
If they remodel this hospital again they should make
another room for you
And put your name on it
Spell it right

From A-Z
And put a extra chair and a bed
You know
Mr and Mrs
Hers and his
The queen and I
See we are one in the same
So what's hurting her
Is paining me
And I still believe
But yesterday
I googled the survival rate
And it made my heart race
Like
Did we catch it too late
Did I ever decide to pray
To just realize the whole time that my mind's been
racing
I been on my knees
And I must've been fatigued
Cause I heard them speak
Please please please
You can't ask for forgiveness when you didn't do
anything
Did I try being patient
Between phone calls doctors nurses pharmacies
Did I try to be patient
Between close calls anxiety and breaking
I got to let my woman know she'll never be a patient
Between house shoes surgeries hospital gowns
Baby I'll never apology cause I seen you naked

Cause I'm naked too
With truth and flaws in awe
Of you
Baby
Cause I'm naked too
To my core my spirit my jaw
I want to speak to you
Baby I'm naked too
With scars involved
Cause I want to save you too
Baby what do we do
Did you ask am I wasting my time
What do you mean
I'm never goin to leave
So baby please please please
Don't ask me for forgiveness
When you didn't do anything

AN ODE TO THE WOMEN OF WUHAN

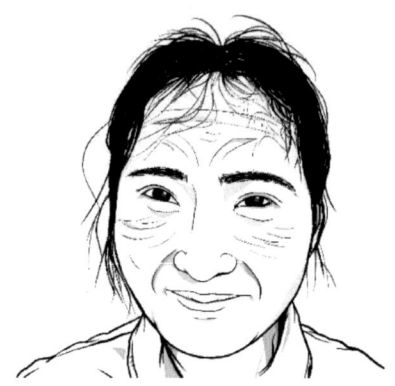

Thank You

For those who think COVID-19
Is a hoax
Even though it spread it's disaster in 2019
Even in its name let us know we were too late to catch
it
Who see it so much as Fake News
That they didn't flinch when the Trump
Administration got its hands on its results
Who fail to mention the hundreds of thousands of
Americans who lost their life
Like those Americans don't have names
Or families attached to them
Pain attached to them
How did we get so far detached from reality

Today I decided to be a writer
And my anxiety wouldn't let me
My vision wouldn't stand strong
It abandoned me
It left me in disarray
It said never instead of not yet
It measured inabilities not success
It told me what it thought
Like I asked a question
Like I asked for a second
Like I have a second
Like I wasn't saying my purpose
Like it was bigger than fear
Like I believe in fear
Can you believe that
Me telling my past that
That I believe in fear
Like I ain't hold more snakes than butterflies
Like I ain't hold more regret than confidence
Like love was enough
Like life is careful
Like we weren't born to stay dangerous
Like life isn't more than jus comfort
That decisions are about your comfort
Like
Is it easy on the eyes
Is it light on the ears
Is it the right tone for you
Is it fitting
Is it fair
Is it Witty

Is it a poem
Does it make your heart race
And if it didn't
How do you know you're alive
How do you know when to breathe
If you never choked
If you never gasped for air
If you never needed to breathe
If you never needed to scream
If you never needed to need
It's like I prayed for you
To stop running
Throu my mind
For a moment
So I can tell you to leave
Cause
If I'm not afraid
Why are you here
How can you stop me
They say weak men lose discipline before they ever
lose battles
This war with you
Is it goin to take for you to be gone for me to be
grateful

And it was gratitude
For the things that are close to me
In spirit and physical
That I found myself next to
More than I'd ever dream of

T.T.T.C.
Third Times The Charm

They say black boys are made men on the streets
And born from hoes
And fall in love with each other's success until a
woman is chose
But baby I chose you
And look
I made a throne of thorns
Is that what Jesus did?
My grandma told me we are God's children
Well maybe he's black too
Cause I feel like he don't see his kids
But look
These rose petals look just like tear drops
And I brought a fountain for you
It came from the same river of 20 aunties eyes when
they nephew died
This will move mountains for you
Wait it's not enough
Do I have to say I hate you for you to love me first
Do I have to take it away for you to know your worth
Do I have to pretend I was never a Slave to free this
curse
Why don't you love me like my mother never did
Disappear and disappoint
And come back every couple years
I know you see with people
They have to see if it's really everlasting
And when the tables turn

It's fine to take a seat and throw another tantrum
Maybe I'll turn another tassel
Graduate from success and find your happiness to be
another hassle
Hold up
Maybe I'm hurt too
And it fills my voice and my spine
To the point I can't walk away or say what's on my
mind
Maybe I'm blind
And it's frustration not love in my eyes
So I only see the shortcomings
And not the blessings in disguise
Maybe I'm wrong too
Well tell me
Who was right about you
Was it everybody else?
Naw there's so much conviction in my point of view
Maybe it's us
Maybe our two wrongs can make a right
If we discussed it with trust
Maybe we can move forward if we stop looking back
at the lies
Maybe we should take it in pride
You know
That one sin that we both love
Maybe it's humility
That can help us to grow love
Maybe we shouldn't fuck with maybe
Just keep it black and white
No need to be color struck

Define your own tone
And know that
We don't have to live there
The past is no home Hold on

Life starts to feel like a dream
Everything is where it needs to be
Watch as strength mimics me
Watch as serenity meets peace
Watch
As time goes forward
I hold hands with seconds

It was a shift
That turned nigga to man
Bitch to royalty
Section 8 to castles
A shift
That black was indeed excellent
That it indeed was currency
In the gold of souls
In the last of humanity
The heart beat of decency
It indeed was a shift
We thought it at once
In unison for once
That it indeed was the corner stone for this worlds
greatest nations
The back that was once stepped on
Now sits up straight
And up right
Cause in this shift
We stopped giving
The power that we have
But we left the love
But we stopped giving
The power that we have
It's like black bodies sweating in the heat
A random black smile in random black places
A cry for liberty
tears of justice
A sense of purpose in place
A sense of purpose in one plate
Like the black

Woman
Man
Child
Spirit
Religion
Vote
Dignity
Divinity
And honor
All
Set on one plate
Like black
Art
Stories
Black writing
All
Mattered in one place
Like it was a Renaissance of black gifts

Clarity

Without a shadow of a doubt
God loves me
Flaws and all
Sometimes the devil on my shoulder
Gives me advice that makes my head nod
That's why
Before I go on my way
I got to burn some sage
Cause I got grace in high places
And demons that can spread wings

She fell in love with symmetry
It's hard to make due
With only half's
Those who are full have to laugh
It's hard to make two
With two pieces who give nothing up
Patience for trust
It gets hard to make two
Of some something
When the first is 1of1
It gets hard to make
That's why most things shift
Like plates
They cause disturbance
They make a motion
Cause it brings change
Moving
More than silence did
More than silence could
It has to bring change
To come together
To become one
Something has to fall
It has to break off
It has to change
To go from
Not loving
To loving
It has to move
You have to walk in it
It should take a shape

Like people can't recognize you
Like you don't seem familiar
Like it's not your features
Like I have seen you before
But you jus seem different
Like the walk is just different
Like it's how you carry yourself
I see someone else now
Like your partner
Walks jus like you
Like it's in unison
Like it's jus one
Like a piece of you
Broke off
And somebody picked it up
Like somebody picked it up
And for once
Two people looked at what was broke
And two people stood still
And two people thought how could they fix it
And great minds did think alike
But different
And it worked both ways
And it was peace in that
And two people walked with half's
Until they piece came back
And from there they started walking
And everyone knew their move was different
And their mood was different
And everyone who wanted examples
Could now see what love is

I can't meet you
 I just don't vibrate that low

I wanted you for so long
I had to realize what my intentions were
I wanted to mold you
I wanted you to be clay for me
To be what I wanted you to be
To transform for me
To become one with my hands and my voice
Like you didn't build yourself
So concerned about wants I forgot about respect
Now I need you to have flesh again

Knowing that
Faith is the same vibe as monogamy

Patience

It's the only way
It heals too much
Like all good things
It helps you enjoy your time
It helps you pace your time
It helps
The doctor that God gave us all
The moment we all look forward to
The same moment that's inside you
Is inside me
That's why it looks so similar when we are rejoicing
things

As men
A lot of us
Love what we do
The skills that we have
And the power and freedom that it produce
That we don't love who we are
That's why we don't know how to be older men

I

Was always told to protect those around me
Rather they be sisters or cousins
To protect those around me
I was prepared for violence then
I've seen men break into pieces
And I've showed those pieces to the world
The world mocks the weak
They point figures and laugh
I guess it's a understood thing
We only hover around winners

I

Didn't know I was tainted
Until I ran into a woman who was pure
Her eyes look like snow to me
She just spoke truth
It was odd to me
How bad I wanted to get closer
How bad I wanted her character
Wishing to dive into her
But not wanting to swap spirits
Just show me how to be simple in this life
Show me how to do right in this life
I see you had a better start than me

I

Wanted to run away from the world
Ever since I seen it
It didn't look pure to me
The surroundings were too muddy
The surroundings were too ugly
And honest
Bold enough to not hide from children
Forceful enough to seep into anyone
Every house I grew up in had more people than rooms
Fingers still crossed
Hoping the friends I have left die from natural causes
In everybody's house
There were more gangsta movies than bibles
My neighbors
Always had more problems and more roaches
So I was thankful
People loved me
So I was thankful
People would slit necks for me
So I was thankful
People would pay debts for me
So I was thankful
So I learned to repay favors
Favors that might not have happened yet
I'd pay first
Off assumptions
Now I need proof
That we lived in dirt for a reason
That we lived in a curse for a reason
Stories have to end better than they start

Your diet is important
Your mind and body
Both need to digest the right things
Both need to exercise
Both need to be tuned
Be careful with them both

I

realized
It's me now
And it's how I react to that
Cause
It's me now and i have to react to that
Cause it's truth that you speak
In the company that we keep
And the honesty that you bring
And the promises that you keep
So i promise from this day forward it's the best of me
and worse of me
So i promise from this day forward
I'm never goin to keep
Bad energy or I'll intent
No Resentment
Jus fellowship
No more replays of what could've been
And be content with what it is
No more he say she say
So
I trust what comes from your lips
And know that bonds are broken from contradictions
And lies do exist
And that people that you know may suffer from too
much flesh
Of my flesh
Cause i attract what i am
And i pose the same threat

I lived on the same frequency
And that we all can fail the same test
And know
That it's God favor or nothing at all
That it's my purpose or nothing at all
That it's you trusting me or nothing at all
That you can get cut bleed and scab
But a scar will tell it all

Genesis

Illmatic remind me of my youth
Followed by the Dogpound with framed pictures of
Noble Drew
Ma dukes in a dashiki
Speaking Haile Selassie quotes while pumping Sade
Adue
It's true
Garvey had my pops walking in a straight line
But pissed how Malcolm changed his life
After 'the white man gave him all that time'

And I'm thinking the same thing as you
What kind of logic is that
Cause where I come from
After studying we always got time to scrap
What's the next thing
Blessed to to have dreams
Where niggas check pockets like a step team and the
alphas back
This one holds from Gresham Road to Flat Shoals
From Metro to Clayco
When Motorola had pounds coming in
But now xan and molly rolling thruough like a
hurricane in town
It's wild
People's moms falling on they knees like a prayer or
FEMA check is going to help clean up they child
And they daughters want lingerie
Even though she could afford one night gown

Then
Players club showed you how to make twenty dollars
in five minutes
Ten years later your favorite quote is who dat on the
pole
And niggas is laying low from a crime they did last
week
Have a argument with they baby momma now you
and the kid can't speak
But you already know
Pressure holds
That's why
When funds get low
You hear the echoes of who you banking with
Real niggas committing fraud and nobody wants to
question this
And pseudos spewing out that they a Malcolm and
not a Martin
But would never shoot back at the police to show them
they life is not more important
Stay tuned on Fox News to see who else Donald
Trump is trying to get deported
Fuck it
I get on IG jus to ease the stress
Just to see baby girl she pressed
Vexed
Feeling like her life is valued at a hundred likes or
more
Got dam
I can't really take no more
From the White House to corporate offices

I wonder if they can hear the screams from the ghetto
there
Or see the teens stuck in peril there
Or see how you can be seventeen years old
With his soul stuck in metal here
Go to school
Got to raise your hand to go to the bathroom still
And turn around leave class commit a crime and
watch a judge give you twenty years
It's 2015
Now a days you got to tell these light voice rappers to
put they fuckin clutches and purses down
Niggas wearing skirts
Can't tell if it's beef or its sweet when he ask 'do you
think I'm the one to fuck around?'
Pause
Can't tell if you Dame Dash or CamRon
Got to question it when you say you want to flip and
put your mans on
Wait Pause
How your skin blacker than liquorish but you still
sweeter than some skittles here
Heaven knows I can't make that joke cause Trayvon
still won't see his 22nd year
I'm rambling
This is ramparts from the graveyard
These old souls be speaking through me
My vocal chords are the stairwell up the Tower of
Babel
No
Like grandma in deep prayer

Dialect slipping from english to tongues
With holy water olive oil and the Holy Ghost in her
heart
Hold on
Is this world still looking for that mind tupac was
destined to spark
But all we left with is niggas not screaming thug life
but pretending to be playing the part
But me
Still Chuck D
Black with the crosshairs aimed at my heart
And when I'm feeling I'm lost
I put in that Illmatic and I get in my spot
It's the Genesis it puts me back in the beginning where
everything starts
Cause
Illmatic remind me of my youth
Followed by the Dogpound with framed pictures of
Noble Drew
Ma dukes in a dashiki speaking Haile Selassie quotes
while pumping Sade Adue
It's true
Garvey had my pops walking in a straight line
But pissed how Malcolm changed his life after the
white man gave him all that time
But still live by the quote
God gets all the glory only the mistakes are mine

Made in the USA
Columbia, SC
27 September 2020